CW00495960

Acknowledgm

Introduction 9

Acknowledgments

This book is an example of a single thought turned into words.

The completion of this work is based on various helpful observations that I had during my visits to multiple places, schools and Ashrams.

I am thankful to my parents whose strong belief in the divine and the values they instilled in me gave me the awareness to realise the simplicity of life.

My son Vivaan Modasiya for being a living example, a subject for study at his young age of 4 years. His dedication in practising meditation assured me that my idea was reliable and meaningful.

I am grateful to have been a part of the PDA Education Assistant course in Edinburgh College – this gave me a broad perspective with which to understand the world of children.

I am also thankful to Catherine Clarke Ouhib for making my work polished and presentable and Lionel Ross who gave me the opportunity to show my work to the world. Their feedback and advice helped me to make the book better.

I believe every energy from nature that has come towards me during this process has given me the strength and positivity to accomplish my work.

Meditation is introspection,
The reflection of yourself through your
inner self,
Observation and evaluation of your
mind's activity,
Recognition of yourself,
The ability to understand the universe
through the simplicity of nature.
The ability to understand the purpose of
one's life.
It enables you to believe in yourself.
The more you simplify your life, the
more you will understand about the subject
of meditation,
as a therapy that brings peace to your
mind, body and soul.

Introduction

Life is a creation of a single thought;
It all begins by a spark of that thought!

This book is a tool that serves to spread my message to all parents, teenagers and people who work in educational settings, in order to create awareness of meditation from an early age.

Briefly, this can positively affect our busy lives by helping to get rid of stress and attachment and helping us achieve self-realisation and build self-esteem.

This book is designed for parents who struggle to dedicate time for their children, parents who are balancing work and family life. With that in mind, I have designed a small book that is easy to read and which offers a quick background on meditation (mindfulness) and its benefits.

Teach your children from a young age the reason of "one existence" and how one can serve humanity. Introduce meditation from a young age, so your child is able to control the mind with consciousness, which in real life means living life with full awareness.

As parents, our main dharma (duty) is to create an awareness of wisdom within our children, so we can have a better world, by steering our future (our children) on the right path. Wanting a better world is a desire that every human being should have, as each of us are part of this large universal living space. As mentioned in Maha Upanishad

"*Vasudhaiva Kutumbakam* – the world is one family". This means inclusion, equality and diversity among humanity. Acceptance and generosity are two of the many mantras of the modest life.

Chapter 1

Meditation

I am not the body neither the mind.

Meditation is a method of controlling and organising our mind. Make your mind work for you instead of being a slave of your own mind.

It's not a hard process nor is it impossible, it just requires discipline and a routine that will gradually give you inner happiness, along with the ability to have patience. If you practise regularly, it will help you to find yourself – your real identity that is perhaps hidden in the fake world of illusion that we call identity.

What is Identity?

Identity is a portrait, a perception that displays in the real world as I. We spend most of our time living within this image which we have gained or modelled from our culture, values and status. But, it is a mere illusion created from our mind.

As we live in this fast-paced environment where everything is seen as just a "quick passage" in our life. We tend to forget the inner essence of our existence and rely only on identity. Therefore, it is important as humans to find our inner self to fulfil our self-actualisation; mediation is the ultimate foundation in recognising that I.

There are two different aspects to identity: personal identity, which is an outer-world description of the person in terms of features, gender, religion, background, qualities and habits. Another is spiritual identity which is related to our inner world. Spiritual identity can be obtained by self-introspection, knowing yourself to the extent that you realise happiness and satisfaction from within. Spiritual identity is our true, pure identity that is the base of our existence.

When we reach this stage, we are able to control our mind totally by being conscious of creating positive thoughts and a harmonious ambience around ourselves.

From my perspective, mediation is a subject that allows for the study of the inner world. It's a subject where science and spirituality are connected to each other. The only difference from other subjects that we learn in educational settings is that meditation requires time to understand and it is a lifelong process. While other subjects can be studied in a limited time, where we can determine the start and end, meditation is eternal and beyond these fixed limits. We all have a natural curiosity about science as it gives us awareness of our external body, the external world. But, the purpose of our existence is to learn about our inner world, which is connected to our soul and supreme-Creator. Listen to your inner voice. Allow yourself a break from the hustle and bustle of a busy life and experience the stillness within you.

Finding Your Inner Self

Finding an inner self is finding our true existence, the true realisation of human beings. It is the ultimate purpose of our life; by delving into the inner world, we will experience true happiness and peace within ourselves. This will lead us into contact with our supreme, the creator, the bright light that conquers the undefined universe.

Over the years, I have had the opportunity to read many religious books: Hindu, Buddhist and Christian. And I have met with wonderful people who taught me about each religion, including Islam. The one common thing that I have understood from all these sources is that humans have most evolved neurological system, the most intelligent species in the world and only they can reach the creator.

For ordinary people who are busy in their day-to-day life, who probably never heard about the power of meditation techniques or if they have, they never tried to practise, and if they practised they did it just a few times and then gave up. It becomes a little hard for them to delve into this ocean of stillness. To be able to experience this nothingness a person should be able to ignore what is happening around him. A disturbed mind caused by reason of samsara (living in a practical world, the cycle of birth and death) such as, family issues, lack of concentration, laziness, social and financial worries: these are the main disruptive causes that put boundaries on exploring ourselves.

The one mantra that applies to overcome all these disruptive causes is to practise techniques of meditation continuously on a daily basis. Initially, you can start this practise for a few minutes and gradually increase the time. It doesn't matter if your physical body is tired or sick the only thing that you need to concentrate is in your spiritual body (inner energy) that is beyond the physical.

Basic Methods of Meditation

One of the techniques that has been used with success by most people is the breathing technique. Sitting in a cross-legged position, with hands resting on thighs and palms facing upwards, breathe in from your right nostril, and breathe out from the left; while breathing in use the help of your finger to close the left nostril. Keep alternating between nostrils using the same technique.

Another method is to focus on thoughts, simply by sitting in a quiet comfortable place, avoid any noise and concentrate on your mind. Analyse what kind of thoughts it is processing. This means in meditating language to ignore negative thoughts and accept positives. In my personal experience, this last method helped me to enter into the meditation process easily, when I was at the beginning of my journey towards Yoga. I used to do this exercise daily, in the morning and that helped me to control my anger and anxiety. It gave me a new approach with which to view the world. It taught me to be passive; it nurtured the empathy inside me, the ability to accept things the way they are.

There are two important facts that we must remember in meditation: one is sitting with a straight **spine** and another is **facing east**, this will allow a flow of positive energy and relaxation of the body's muscles.

*The **Spine** is a tool that connects the human body with the universe itself.* An erect and flexible spine is essential for the development of the mental and physical aspects of the human body. Therefore, most of us prefer to sit upright with a straight spine while doing any study, work or even reading, this helps the mind to easily capture and absorb the information.

A simple exercise done for a few minutes can transform your quality of life: this can work as an energy charger for the whole day. It will give stability to the mind, enabling positivity around you.

Feeding your mind with meditation will allow you to be motivated and be in harmony with yourself – be your own best companion. Nobody can understand your inner "I" more than yourself. Give time to yourself.

Unfortunately, some of us have misunderstood the meaning of "stillness" as we think it means stilling the mind from processing thoughts. Our misconception is that I am mind. Yogic language explains that I am not the mind nor the body. So to experience stillness, you cannot stop your mind, let it work naturally, that is its duty the same as you cannot stop your blood moving into different veins. The only thing that you can do is to focus towards a single point. Then you will experience that stillness. To achieve this level requires a lot of patience and time. Until then stick with the basic technique that will eventually take you towards this beautiful journey of exploring yourself.

There are no age or health restrictions when it comes to practising meditation. Anybody can do this exercise at any time of the day that suits his or her lifestyle. However, mornings and evenings are the best times to practise as sunrise and sunset create a peaceful atmosphere. Every individual is different and unique so the choices can vary. It is essential that you listen to your body's needs and comforts.

Chapter 2

The Influence of Places & Nature in Meditation

Tune in to your conscious and subconscious mind through meditation.

The Effect of Sunrise

Sunrise has many functions: it offers a panoramic view that enchants our eyes, along with healing treatments for our body, mind and soul.

Sunrise has the power to divert our mind from many "tensions" and enables us to focus only on the rising sun. Try to sit in a place where you can see the rising sun. Capture that moment, absorb the fresh ambience created through the shining rays, let them pass through your body and fulfil their natural therapeutic duty. It is like a scanner that rejuvenates all your dead, tired cells. Sunlight is one element of the nutrition required for our body and mind to keep fresh and alive.

Whenever natural marvels occur, unconsciously our mind tends to concentrate only on that moment; it is overwhelmed by extraordinary natural events. Take advantage of the natural circumstances that calm your mind. Embrace these moments that are present every day of your life: by listening to the musical sound of the birds, waves and wind or inhaling and exhaling the air in different seasons of the year, feel the scent of each season. Embrace the charismatic nature around you.

The Advantages of Practising Meditation on the Night of a Full Moon.

The moon has an especial connection with the mind, therefore meditating on the night of a full moon gives rise to an opportunity. Everything that you do on that day enhances your logical or illogical qualities.

The human body is made up of five elements: water (blood), fire (heat), air (breath), earth (bones) and space (consciousness). The energy that runs in our body through these elements is known as *Prana Shakti* or vital force; any imbalance in the five elements can bring imbalance in our vital force, leading to sickness and diseases. Therefore, our body suffers when even slight changes occur in this large cosmos; the human body is the fruit of the universe itself. Anything can affect our lifestyle, even floods, droughts, the ozone, or eclipses. Everything affects us knowingly or unknowingly, in our inner world as well as in our outer world.

The yogis strongly believe in this connection between the universe and the human body. Everything in this cosmos relates to each other. The impact of full Moon can create high tides in the sea similarly, it can change emotional behaviour patterns into humans. If you cannot dedicate time for yourself every day, then the day of a full moon is an opportunity for you to rise yourself in order to enhance the good qualities residing within you through meditation.

Enchanting Kashi

Kashi – known as Banaras or Varanasi, is a beautiful, most ancient city, spiritual with a vibrant atmosphere. This divine and mystic city is located on the banks of the river Ganga. According to the ancient Puranas, this city is beloved by the god Shiva. Yog (meditation) is the spirit of Kashi. One cannot escape feeling the radiant yogic atmosphere here. Everything is enchanting. It is an ideal place for those who are seeking simplicity and wisdom. It is a place of worship and belief in the existence of the supreme.

This place has a huge influence on the practise of meditation, especially when you are on the initial stage of this journey; Kashi made an incredible mark on my spiritual journey.

This place influenced me by enriching my spiritual knowledge. It was a soul-elevating experience. The journey to Kashi changed my perspective on life. When you visit Kashi, the first thing that you are told to do is to have a bath in the sacred river Ganga to "purify your soul". It is one of the Hindu beliefs. Then we moved on to perform *Surya Namaskar* at about six o' clock in the morning in the presence of a heavenly, radiant sunrise; this was followed by a boat trip over the river Ganga to our main destination, Vishwanath temple. The temple is dedicated to the eternal Yogi, the omnipresent, the positive energy that flows in all his creatures, the Shiva. This temple is a place of pilgrimage for Hindus. Kashi is also known as the place that gives *moksha* (free from birth cycles).

Shiva – the creator of Yog, also symbolised as Shivalinga. My definition of Shivalinga is based on humankind: the upper part of the Shivalinga represents the human body (physical body), while the base of Linga represents the essence of existence (spiritual body) and meditation serves as a connection between these two bodies. Although, the meaning of Shivalinga according to Puranas is one of the forms of Shiv and Shakti, my definition is the fruit of my study on Shivalinga through my concentration – meditation.

Nobody can perfectly answer your questions. Only you can find answers by digging to the deepest level within yourself, in order to find the purest version of your truth. Humans tend to wear different masks to fit into society such as, personality, identity and image, but all these are mere illusions. The purest, most honest version of yourself lies behind all those masks that block the ability to recognise our true essence of being.

Everybody has the potential to draw answers from themselves without submerging into someone else's beliefs and opinions. Meditation is a blessed gift a humankind; we need to explore it in order to live a meaningful life. For many years, we have wrongly connected meditation to the sages, monks and spiritual followers, but it is a human truth, a reality that we hardly explore due to lack of awareness. Unfortunately because of this unawareness we have become slaves of our own mind. We tend to follow our mind's instructions, instead of guiding the mind with good thoughts. We need to have complete control of our mind and body. For example when we have a guest in our home, we are supposed to tell them how things work in our home according to our own lifestyle and rules. But if this order is reversed and the guest becomes the authority in the home then the chances are you will be excluded from your own home.

Stop grumbling about what you have not achieved so far, stop running in races in order to compete with millions of people, this won't give you the glory of freedom. Try instead to compete with your own capabilities in order to get the best from yourself. We humans are like diamonds, the more you sharpen yourself, the brighter and shinier you become. In the yogic world this means, the more you meditate, the more you will control your mind, the wiser you will become.

Many times, we see in the media, people asking spiritual leaders what is the purpose of their life? Before you ask this question, have you ever thought about it by yourself; have you ever taken the time to do some introspection of yourself through your inner self? If not, then why to bother other people with unanswered questions, living in false expectations that someone else can solve my problems. Only this "I" has the power to guide and nurture my life. Therefore, only I can study myself in detail, only I have the permission to enter into my subconscious and get solutions to my dilemmas. Understand what is happening in the large universe inside you by experiencing silence; listen to every breath, pulse and organ function in you. And then you will get enlightenment of your existence.

What Is Self?

Self is the Atman that is beyond any form. It is the life made by the Universe itself: a pure energy that flows inside us.

How to Listen Your Inner Voice?

You need to sit in a quiet place, for some time, and dedicate that time to yourself. Be consistent, be a good observer of your feelings and emotions. Try to make yourself happy, by believing in yourself. This quality of stillness is present in every human, we just need to dig it out from our within and restore it to our practical world. Be conscious of your subconscious. The subconscious is the powerful part of our main machine (the mind). It has the power to enlighten you or it can drag you into the dark.

Humans are the most intellectual species on the planet. We are gifted with a mind that makes wonders. Nothing is impossible for humans. They are capable of anything according to their desire. If they desire to spend holidays on the moon (with the flow of new technology it's possible it will be a future holiday destination) then most likely, nothing in this universe can stop them. Humans are discovering more and more day after day. Why not start to discover our inner world that is as undefined as the universe.

Running towards success, chasing your dreams are all good causes in life. But don't be so busy in all that materialistic achievement to the extent that you ignore yourself. Be attached to your internal world, in spite of the outer; that's the true meaning of being independent.

Once you understand the I within you, then you won't feel the necessity of having luxurious holidays or a luxurious living standard. Everything around you will become as blissful and peaceful as what you experience on those wonderful holiday islands. The mistake that we make is to find peace (an internal feeling) in the outside world, through holiday destinations. That's the reason that whenever we come back from holidays, we are more tired than before, and the mind is still seeking peace and we think again about booking another holiday. It is like an endless process.

Once you achieve this stage of finding peace within you, then you probably won't need as many breaks from family and work. And if you do go to explore another place, it will serve as a learning journey for you. You will be able to understand the nature and the humanity more strongly than before.

Chapter 3
Introduction of Meditation from an Early Age

A child's healthy mind should be a primordial need.

Meditation provides holistic development for the external and internal body of the human being. The best time to start meditation is from a young age. Studies have proven that our cognitive development starts from birth. At the age of three, toddlers start nursery; they are ready to learn; they have the ability to memorise rhymes and songs, as well as follow instructions. This can be the best time to implement basic meditation techniques and Yoga exercises in their routine. This will help grow their awareness of how to sit quiet for a period of time and gradually will enhance their curiosity about it.

There are plenty of private Yoga classes for children. Why not establish this in mainstream schools and other educational settings where every child can benefit from it without parents having to pay exorbitant fees?

There are many reasons that make me keen to convince adults to introduce the magical yet natural therapy of controlling the mind to their children.

A child's brain is completed by seven years of age. So, anything we plant in their mind up to that age takes a strong root. Even experts in the field of science and spirituality agree on this point. So, humans can use this benefit in their practical life, in order to better understand situations around them, and be able to make decisions appropriately in response to the circumstances.

Children's minds are framed by this programme which means behaviours, actions and attitudes that have been implemented by their families and surroundings. And the root of the programme is attached to the subconscious mind. As we know, the subconscious mind has a huge impact on the function of the mind. The subconscious mind rules over the conscious mind. So, anything that we must delete from this programme has to be deleted from the subconscious. Meditation is that therapy that enables the cleansing of the mind. It allows us to organise our mind. It is a healing process to cure all negativity inside our mind.

Therefore, most of the time, children from poor families tend to think low and children from rich families tend to think high. They get this perception from their family's influence and surrounding environment. They tend to define their world using that false perception.

Many innovative schemes are used nowadays for children's wellbeing and education. It's always beneficial for a child to get new opportunities where they can develop their skills and experience. But meditation has not been part of the programme in mainstream schools and nurseries where all children can reap the benefits of it. Meditation will enhance their hidden capabilities, it will teach them to believe in themselves. Essentially, they will discover themselves and overcome their fears through it. Meditation does not require any expensive resources; it can be done using basic natural resources that are already available at homes, schools and nurseries. The only requirement is a quiet, clean, bright place (this can be in classrooms, gym halls, living rooms, bedrooms and so on).

While studying to become an Education Support Assistant in Edinburgh I had the opportunity to learn about the education system in Scotland in detail. I came across different policies and initiatives during the course. Mainly they are strongly focused on children's education and wellbeing. But, the one where meditation fits in is the Curriculum for Excellence.

Curriculum for Excellence's main aim is to help children and young people to be successful learners, responsible citizens, confident individuals and effective contributors.

Curriculum for Excellence gives teachers and students freedom in achieving their educational goals. It is diversified, allows the use of various resources adaptable to children's needs and requirements. The simple activity of playing with dough can enhance various aspects of child development. While playing with dough a child is developing his cognitive, physical and emotional skills as well as language development.

With this freedom to do the best for children to make them realise their potential, it is worth implementing meditation in an educational setting, as it has the same purpose as the above policy. The subject of meditation will allow children to not only explore their outer world, but to recognise their inner world – the stillness. For a person who is comfortable with himself, who can understand himself, who can recognise himself, anything will be easy to achieve in the outer world. Unfortunately, the education that children receive nowadays helps them solely to explore their skills and capacities without recognising the existence of their inner self.

Through meditation, we learn concentration; that is one of the essential qualities required to be successful in our studies and in life generally. Concentration is the breath of a successful human. To achieve any goals in your life you need to be focused. A clear mind is necessary; this can be achieved through wisdom and awareness which are the main outcomes of meditation.

The educational setting is a place of knowledge and wisdom – the best place to introduce meditation to children's lives. It is essential for them to understand the importance of nothingness, to experience stillness by being quiet for some time. The importance of giving time to yourself, to enjoy your own company, because only you can be your best "friend" or companion for your entire life. Meditation is a charger of positive energy in our body and mind.

For teachers who have concerns about their pupil's wellbeing, or their own wellbeing (in order to prevent headaches at the end of the day), a simple 15 minutes of meditation before you start the class can be a solution. If practising daily, then the results will be noticed easily.

The Role of a Good Teacher?

A teacher is not only the most influential person in a student's life, but also the eyes to show them the real world. A true teacher is one who can create empathy with his students, one who can understand and care about their feelings and needs, one who can come down to the level of the students, by this generating a good mutual relationship, based on honesty and respect.

One needs to experience meditation personally in order to guide children to the practise. This can be done individually or by groups. Integrate meditation, as part of your culture, as part of your family's goals in the same way you would choose a day for a family gathering or a routine time for breakfast or dinner; do the same with meditation. Dedicate one time slot where the whole family can just experience stillness all around. This will act as an incentive to your children to accept this as part of their daily routine and gradually it will become a habit, just like other basic habits that we as parents nurture in our children such as, teeth brushing or having a bath (essential hygiene). In the same way meditation works as a deep internal cleansing of our mind and body.

It's human nature that we tend to find solutions to our problems in the external world when they can be solved by ourselves. We tend to become so vulnerable to the extent that we dedicate our happiness and peace to someone else. This is one of the immature habits that we nurture throughout our life. Why do we feel happy when we get good news and instantly feel sad when we receive bad news? Because, we label everything around us as bad and good, according to our point of view and vague knowledge about everything we see around us. If we simply accept things the way they are then life will be much easier to live. This means, accepting myself the way I am. Recognising my qualities and incapacities and saying to myself: "this is me and I am OK with it". When we say every individual is different and unique this literally means accepting every human as he or she is. Don't try to change them. Most problems arise when we start to change the nature of things or people around us. Most of the conflicts in relationships or even in the workplace are fruits of expectations: "others should do it the way I want". Once we overcome feelings of attachment, expectation and dependency then acceptance will be the only nature remaining in us.

Unknowingly, we all practise meditation daily. Meditation means when a human mind practises concentration. When we meditate, we concentrate on our within through the activity of breathing. On a daily basis, we do activities that need lots of concentration, for example reading, writing, playing sport, cooking or simply having a conversation with a friend (we become active listeners and focused on what the other person is saying). Concentration is life itself, it is present in everything we do. Through concentration we can organise and understand our within world (inner self).

Meditation will make children flourish, in a way that will change their perspective on thinking and viewing the world around them. When practising from the age of three, by the time of their teenage years (the stage where most conflicts start between parents and children), they will be able to make the right decisions, choose the right circle of friends and avoid negativity around them.

As a parent no other gift can be as precious for their children than the ability to organise their mind through meditation. It will be an eternal gift that will be with them for their entire life. This will certainly, decrease parent's worries as it will prevent children making bad choices or following the wrong path in life.

Believe in yourself, because this self is your only permanent companion that will lead you to achieve all your desires.

How Meditation Can Positively Affect Children with Additional Support Needs

Every individual is unique, we need to respect and accept the way each one is created.

We as humans are not perfect, we all suffer some kind of disability, no one can escape this: whether it's physical, mental, social or materialistic and the list goes on...so, jumping to conclusions on what is normal and abnormal is not an intelligent attitude.

A physical mechanism can go wrong in the body and that function is perhaps then determined by others. But nobody can steal the ability to decide how to live within yourself.

Meditation can be a great strength for children with ASN. It helps them to work through their "inner world". Because physical disabilities can only cause barriers in their "outer world". Meditation will give them the concept of complete realisation by training their mind, ignoring their physical challenges and concentrating only on their inner capabilities.

One who understands his own imperfections is the one who truly understands the meaning of equality among humanity.

Meditation not only provides a holistic approach to every aspect of life, but it also, teaches us that we are all equal in the journey of seeking the truth of life, true happiness. Here, we are all disabled from that wisdom of awareness and the path is the same for all of us, it does not matter whether you can speak, see, walk or run. There is only one language, the language of silence to follow; listening and inner sight are also necessary. So, physical attributes won't give you an advantage; we must all start this journey from the beginning.

Once you get further on your yogic journey, you will realise the importance of detachment – *sadhana* the simplicity of life. For common humans it is difficult to reach this stage as we are attached to what is around us so strongly, that we even forget about that "I" within us. But this quality can be found easily in people who have additional needs as they are already living with absences and can still survive without filling those gaps. This is known as overcoming that need – detachment.

As a parent help your children to awaken their inner sight, which is much brighter and more honest than the outer world. Give them the confidence to believe in themselves.

Meditation Can Prevent Bullying and Behaviour Issues

The effects of meditation that I have described can also create a positive influence in preventing bullying.

Most people have suffered from bullying in their childhood and even in adulthood; sometimes the marks of bullying can remain forever.

What is bullying?

Bullying is an activity practised by humans that can cause embarrassment or discomfort to another person. This can lead to suffering and feelings of being neglected. Unfortunately, children have an awareness of this malicious behaviour from a young age, due to their surroundings. Children are the reflection of society; their actions are influenced by observing their environment. It is an unappropriated behaviour that has no purpose or meaning, so it should be removed from the root, a root that has unfortunately made a home in many children's minds.

For children who are suffering from behaviour issues, this ancient therapy can work miracles as it enables them to have control over different situations with a calm mind, avoiding restlessness and stress that is caused by a heavy environment around them.

Most of the time in our society, behaviour issues are treated as a medical condition therefore the right steps are not taken to guide children correctly. This can lead to impaired behaviours over time, which can be harmful for them as well as for those around them.

Preventing behaviour issues from an early age enables children to make their future safe, and so society can be safe. We should not forget that as adults our main responsibility is to nurture appropriately our "future" – the children. They are the tomorrow, so the world will depend on them.

Chapter 4

Mind & Body: A Journey from Conscious to Subconscious

Think you're happy, believe you're happy and happiness will be forever with you.

The conscious and subconscious are the main programmes of the human's main computer – the mind. Nurturing the mind with positive thoughts is the main responsibility of a human being.

Everything that you do or be, will be planned only by your mind.

Meditation has the power to balance your conscious and subconscious mind.

What Are Thoughts?

Thoughts are ideas that we create in our mind. Some transform into acts that we experience personally or observe through other beings. These experiences are memorised in our mind and feelings become attached to them. These feelings can be merely superficial or deeper. But all of them emerge in our conscious mind first. The one that becomes a deeper feeling is the one that stays in our subconscious mind. So, how I can prove this mechanism of feelings: what are superficial feelings? These are connected to someone or something that is not directly connected to us as an individual. For example when we see an advertisement appealing for food or financial support for children in poor countries. Our mind immediately sends us a message saying this is sad, but it is natural for this to happen due to the circumstances in which the children are growing up. So, we try our best to help them, as they are part of humanity. We don't become strongly attached to this feeling.

Deeper feelings become connected when we see someone from our family suffering from any disease (at this time, the mind sends us a message saying this is our priority in life). We get so involved with them because we think our life depends on them and so we need them to be heathy. This, we define as a strong attachment feeling that gets absorbed by our subconscious mind. Anything printed within our subconscious mind works like a disc that plays 24 hours a day in order to make us aware of its existence. This function of the mind goes beyond our control day by day and it starts to cause us stress, anxiety and headaches – the feeling that we have "a heavy stone on our head". But unconsciously, we are the creators of this as we feed our subtle mind with false attachments.

If you analyse carefully, the role of the conscious mind is purely to absorb all the outer/inner observations. But it is the subconscious mind that categorises those observations, assigns a meaning to them and puts them into actions. So the subconscious is the ultimate storage point where thoughts flourish without any acknowledgment of whether they are positive or negative. Therefore, it is essential that we generate new positive habits that allow us to rise to the highest potential in our lives. And meditation plays a powerful role in changing negative habits to positive ones.

What Is Attachment?

Attachment is to be a dependant of someone or something; in yogic language attachment is exclusiveness from everything around you and inside you. Therefore, attachment restricts our ability for self-recognition.

Because of this attachment, most of us limit our lives: our work, family, society, norms and rules are boundaries that forbid us to go beyond in search of true happiness. One thing is clear, the more we achieve the more restless we become in the constant search for having more and more. Because we still believe that seeking materialistic things will make us the happiest person in the whole universe. But we forget to stop for a while and say I am happy with what I have achieved. Everything that I acquire is enough for me to survive happily in this outer world. One who understands this simple law of nature – the acceptance of simplicity in life is one who gets to walk the real path towards true happiness. The more you seek from your inner world, the more confident you become with yourself. At this stage you can contribute to the welfare of humanity, or simply to those around you, unselfishly. At this stage you will acquire total control over your conscious and subconscious mind. Anything that we do beyond our self-interest becomes a fruit for eternal pleasure.

How to Minimise the Risk of Anxiety and Stress?

The media has a big influence on us nowadays. Most of our anxiety and stress are caused by the news that we receive every day by social media. We need to be sensible in filtering the news. Morning habits should be dedicated to treating your inner self, preparing yourself for the day ahead. Allow time to think about what your priorities are for the day and how you will accomplish them. It is like setting baby-step goals. Allow your mind time to absorb the enchanting, silent atmosphere in the morning. Enrich your mind and body with the vibrant energy that will make you lively throughout your day.

But most of us do completely differently to what has been prescribed to us by nature for a healthy life. We humans always like to go against nature and therefore, we suffer the worst consequences that we do not have the ability to overcome. We have a daily morning routine that comprises waking up and instantly checking the mobile next to the bed. We can hardly open our eyes, but we force them to visualise the barbarous, unnecessary news that damages not only our eyesight, but also destroys our mind (slowly, so we aren't even aware). Our mind and body are very delicate gifts that we own from nature, so it is obvious that to make them healthy and strong we need to feed them with nature itself. Taking in fresh air while walking in fresh green grass, is not only beneficial for our eyesight but also, it relaxes the mind. For those who are lucky to live on islands or tropical places where the weather is pleasant most of the year, they can experience this beauty of walking early in the morning and notice the positive effects that this can have on the body, mind and soul. Although in places where winter reigns most of the year, we still are blessed to have some months in spring and summer where we can make the most of this time and feel the difference in ourselves. Another simple option is to make your house comfortable, with some natural fresh plants that can contribute to a healthy life. Make your own place delightful to the extent that you receive harmony and joy from it. Start your morning naturally with nature around, news that we receive is all an illusion made by humans and these are the main obstacles to our happiness, instead make your mornings as bright as the sun. Every morning is a sign that we are still alive. Treasure this life as a unique gift.

Allow yourself to live in the present, do not burden yourself with the past or the future. Accept the present as the divine gift and make each moment happier by living it meaningfully.

So, use your present precisely and wisely by worshipping and concentrating on your Atman (inner self).

Chapter 5
First Steps Towards Meditation

Listen to your inner voice

When I attempted to start Yoga, I started first with meditation, as I strongly believe that anything that you do requires attention and concentration. So, I started to practise breathing techniques to get myself focused. I used to do inhalation and exhalation exercises for ten minutes and five Surya Namaskar. In the beginning I had difficulty controlling my thoughts as I was trying to "stop" my mind which is impossible, unaware of the fact that I was supposed to ignore my thought process and to focus only on breathing. Then I started to sit quietly and chant the word AUM, breathing normally, my focus was only on uttering the AUM sound. This technique helped me to get my mind relaxed after meditation.

The Definition of OM

AUM is a divine word and the purest word in the spiritual universe. We know it as OM (as it is spelled in many books).

Whenever we hear the word AUM we immediately connect it with Hinduism, as this is the word chanted by Indian sages since long ago.

According to the Upanishads (Hindu Vedic literature), AUM is the first ever sound made in the universe. It represents the reality, the internal connection with the cosmos. It is the breath itself that helps to recognise the "Self". AUM is the Present.

The one thing that motivated me was the fact that, after every meditation session I used to feel a calmness in my mind. So, I started to practise more often without worrying about thoughts. Whenever I got lost in thoughts, I used to bring my mind back to meditation. After some time, I felt that my mind was producing fewer thoughts while I was practising meditation than before. My capacity for concentration was stronger than before. Gradually, I achieved the stage where I was comfortable sitting for an hour or more, enjoying the nothingness and experiencing the harmony within myself. Concretisation of pure silence and pure awareness.

Controlling the mind is all about controlling thoughts. Let all the thoughts generate in your mind, but you choose which one to ignore and which one to retain – as simple as ignoring negative thoughts and accepting positive ones. As you accept positive thoughts this will produce another positive thought and so on. So essentially, we need to be aware of what we choose. Before taking any decision, think about the inputs that thought can create when turning into an action. If it will bring sorrow or unhappiness for others or even for yourself then ignore it. It is like cutting the damaged root of any unhealthy plant. Just implement thoughts that can contribute to your happiness and the happiness of others. This proves that if a person seeks happiness then he must give happiness to others. Everything that we do gets multiplied in this large universe and comes back to us many times over; remember that, what we sow is what we reap, the basic law of nature.

The secret to having an abundance of joy resides in spreading a little happiness in everyday life.

The Meaning of Happiness

The definition of the word Happiness:

H= health

A= appreciation

P= power

P= positivity

I= introspection

N= natural

E= energy

S= successful

S= selfless

Silence is the rhythm of life. One who acknowledges this, will achieve the purpose of life that lies in inner happiness.

Meditation teaches us to experience the silence. The power of silence flourishes once you have a healthy mind and body. And for this, a healthy diet is essential. Our diet defines us, it makes not only our body, but it also reflects in our thoughts. Healthy means eating from the source, fresh and seasonal. Fresh food has minerals and vitamins that enrich our body with positive energy. I know how difficult it is to make fresh food, in today's world, when most of us hardly get time for breakfast or lunch and dinner is the only proper meal. So, we should at least try to make some effort in order to prevent many diseases and doctor's appointments. As we know an unhealthy mind and body does not give happiness to us or to those around us. It is worth changing all your packaged foods to fresh ones. It will be more time-consuming to prepare a healthy meal, but soon it will become a habit. Once you get into the habit of eating everything fresh then believe me no "packaged food" will taste as appetising. Add more greenery to your diet. Vegetables and fruits are made to be consumed by humans, so make the most of it. The more "green" (vegetables) you add into your food the "greener" your life will become. Remember, everything that we eat becomes part of us; therefore, consuming nutritious food enables us to be healthy. One who feels in good physical and mental condition can achieve the wisdom of inner happiness. A good diet is a source of good and positive thoughts. Your thoughts and appearance are the mirror of your diet. It can tell your food habits. The food you eat becomes the human you are.

Basic Tips for a Healthy Diet

Make your diet more colourful and fresh by using a variety of vegetables and fruits. This food is easy to digest as it takes less time to pass through the human body. While food such as bread, grains and meat take longer to digest.

Swop your big portions for small. As an example, if you are hungry do not eat two or three apples at a time but try to eat a variety of different foods such as, one apple and a handful of almonds, by doing this you will have different types of vitamins that enable your body to function better. Eating the same food in big quantities will have a negative impact on your body. Integrate food that is good in quality and variety in your daily routine.

Drinking plenty of water enables your body to stay hydrated and also works as an internal cleanser.

Follow a food timetable, for example if you have breakfast at 8 am then try to take your last meal by 8 pm. By following this every day, the night-time hours will work as **intermittent fasting hours**: when your body is going through digestion and the healing process. During this process the body itself absorbs all the essential vitamins from the food and discharges all the toxins from every organ as waste. Allowing your body to heal naturally will prevent many of the diseases (such as constipation, cholesterol, Asthma) that are caused by bad eating habits.

Healthy digestion is important, and this occurs only when you are eating in a happy state of mind, appreciating and being thankful for what you have on your plate. Mealtimes should be performed religiously by feeling every *paladar* (taste) of the food.

Last but not least, chew the food in order to make it the most liquid consistency possible, to allow quick and easy digestion.

It is important for children to have a balanced diet from a young age; this will prevent future health problems, and also help them to achieve their cognitive, educational and physical growth potential.

The body is our god-gifted *sojourn* (temporary stay), it is our duty and priority to make it clean every day, the same way we clean or decorate our house in order to make our living space peaceful and organised, not allowing bacteria and moulds degrade it. It is essential to feel good and healthy from the inside and the outside will automatically reflect this. Only when you are healthy in your mind and body will you be comfortable and confident with yourself.

Chapter 6

The Benefits of Meditation and Yoga in Preventing and Curing Diseases

Awake the doctor within you; be your own healer.

The Mind Can Heal the Body

We all have an inner doctor within us. An inner healer that knows best how to prevent and cure most diseases. What we need to do is just as simple as listening to our intuition.

It also relates to the yogic world as if you believe in yourself as a happy person, then you are – the power of believing, the power of positive thoughts.

How the Mind Can Heal the Body

The relaxation response is where blood pressure, heart rate, digestive functioning and hormonal levels are all in their normal state. At this time our body releases healing hormones such as, serotonin, oxytocin, dopamine and endorphins. These are natural cures for most of the diseases that we encounter in everyday life. They help us to build up our immune system. But, these healing benefits can only be achieved if the body produces a relaxation response. As most of us have so many complaints nowadays, regarding family life, relationship problems, work problems and financial problems this leads to constant stress and depression. Therefore, our body more often produces a stress response rather than a relaxation response. So, what is a stress response? It's when the body thinks it is in danger and starts to release hormones and chemicals to fight that danger, this is called the fight-response. Once the threat has passed, the body should be able to shift into a relaxation response, otherwise the hormones and chemicals released by the stress response start to have negative consequences in our body.

Meditation is the natural therapy that enables you to produce a relaxation response in your mind and body. Programme your mind with a flow of vibrant, positive energy within you, because it's only YOU that can repair yourself totally and completely from any ailment.

Meditation is a holistic therapy; it is a bridge that helps us to overcome whatever is lacking in our lives: this can be physical, emotional, psychological or social.

The key to a happy and healthy life is a combination of meditation with Yoga exercises and a healthy diet. Living a life based in simplicity and being generous with whatever you have.

As Gandhi said once: the world has enough for every being's need, but not enough for the greedy.

Yoga Asanas for Children

Including Yoga exercises in your daily life prevents diseases, increases flexibility and strengthens the muscles. It rejuvenates the dead cells and increases the flow of lively energy in your body and mind.

As we know, Yoga asanas (postures also called pranayama) are beneficial for everyone. Food, water and air are the three baselines of the human body. Oxygen (pure air) plays a vital role in the body's growth, it passes into the lungs and makes the blood pure, however the nose is the best access point for oxygen to enter the body. Therefore, breathing techniques are always a priority in any pranayama exercise.

A child can benefit greatly from this ayurvedic therapy of wellness, especially those who suffer from developmental delays, or other health conditions such as, autism, cerebral palsy, Down syndrome or hyperactive conditions. Yoga enables body awareness, increasing the flow of blood in the entire body, along with improving flexibility, coordination and strength; it enhances positive physical and mental growth. The following are some basic asanas that can be practised at an early stage. Each asanas has multiple benefits for the human body, however only a few benefits are mentioned:

- **Kapalbati** – provides oxygen to the body; helps to prevent and cure obesity; improves blood circulation.

- **Anulom – vilom** – improves concentration; helps to cure neurological and gastric problems.

- **Titli (Butterfly) asana** – helps to calm the body and mind and improves balance.

- **Brahmari** – helps to cure mental tensions, hypertension and enhances concentration.

- **Surya Namaskar** – improves learning capabilities and memory; improves sleep patterns; increases energy.

There are several other asanas that help children in achieving their milestones that we can easily have access to nowadays through the media, internet or even Yoga classes.

Conclusion

The right education and guidance are so important for children to enable them to become independent emotionally and materially. It offers a glimpse of the world around them; this growth helps them to become good human beings and be able to serve humanity and preserve the nature around them. One who can understand this basic aspect of life is one who has attained universal knowledge.

As we know, people are suffering from more stress and depression nowadays, which sometimes leads to major diseases. As a result, we end up blaming life for all the obstacles coming our way, forgetting the reality that life is the most precious gift that we have ever received. Life itself is a happiness. Life is an ongoing, infinite teaching on the self. Respect yourself, by respecting, caring and nurturing your life and the lives of others around you. This simple thought can transform into an action providing multiple solutions for many sorrows and sufferings. As you believe in yourself, so you will believe in others, as everybody is unique with different potentials; that is the real fairness, the real belief in equality among humankind.

As a parent start from educating yourself and changing your habits. Children are a mere reflection of their parents and society, therefore don't expect them to change first; it is you who have to model the changes for them to follow gradually and patiently.

Happiness is the real status of the stable mind.

Happiness is the experience from which we find our Self. It is indeed the real nature of the Self.

Concentration is a foundation of life,

The beginning of a journey,

The ending of a search;

The infinite search towards enlightenment,

The grasp of the knowledge attained by wisdom;

Concentration is existence,

The thread that unifies the I with the supreme;

Concentration is infinite contentment,

The real satisfaction of realisation.

Concentration is the ultimate achievement.